Internet for Ge

CU00894326

David Hawgoo[d]

Published by
David Hawgood
26 Cloister Road
Acton
London W3 0DE
England

Distributed by
Family Tree Magazine
61 Great Whyte
Ramsey
Huntingdon
Cambs PE17 1HL.
Phone 01487 814050
Fax 01487 711361
Web address:
www.family-tree.co.uk

ISBN 0 948151 19 6

First published 1996
Second edition 1999

Printed in England by
Parchment (Oxford) Ltd

CONTENTS

The author has pages
on the World Wide Web at:
http://www.Hawgood.co.uk

Those pages include links to Web sites mentioned in this book. Note that World Wide Web addresses are generally given in this book without the initial "http://". The address above would just be given as www.Hawgood.co.uk.

INTRODUCTION

The **Internet** is a facility which lets you use information and programs on thousands of computers across the world, and exchange messages with millions of computer users.

This book concentrates on what you can get out of the Internet to assist your hobby of family history. It is mainly for genealogists considering use of the Internet. It is also for people who are established users of Internet who want to know what types of information and service are available for genealogy. Newspapers and magazines give news about developments in the ways of using the Internet, which changes rapidly.

In writing this book I have been greatly helped by other family historians. I thank Brian Randell in particular for detailed comments on a draft of the book, and also with his colleagues for starting the UK and Ireland Genealogical Information service GENUKI. I thank friends from the Society of Genealogists Computer Committee and FFHS Publications for comments and suggestions, and readers of *Family Tree Magazine* who responded positively to my challenge "Have you actually obtained anything useful from the Internet".

Some electronic addresses from this book are on my own pages on the World Wide Web. Addresses can be copied from there, or used directly as links. I hope this will reduce the number of complicated addresses readers have to type when starting to use Internet. My World Wide Web address is printed on the title page of this book.

WHAT YOU CAN DO - CATEGORIES

Email - electronic mail, private messages

To use email you type a message at your computer, add the email address of the correspondent, and tell your computer to connect to the telephone network and send the message. It is stored temporarily in a central computer, but it is a private message, not made available to other users. The message is transferred to your correspondent's computer next time it is connected to Internet. It can be displayed, printed and stored. Email is simple, and enormously useful once you have a group of friends or colleagues or family also on Internet.

Conferences with public messages:
Mailing list, Discussion forum, Usenet, Newsgroup

For all of these, the idea is to simulate a public notice board with a defined subject. Anyone who has subscribed to the group can put a message on the board (i.e. in the computer); you can reply either privately to the individual enquirer, or into the public area for all to see. The general term for this type of operation is **conferencing**. A variant is Internet Relay Chat, where a group of people with common interests are all on-line together and exchange messages.

Extend your computer

Email and conferencing are interactions with other people, sitting at their computers. Just about everything else you can do on Internet could be done on your own computer - if it was big enough and contained the data and programs available on thousands of computers around the world, and was constantly receiving the latest versions of every type of information. Sometimes it is difficult to tell whether the computer which puts information on your screen is the one on your desk, one on a local network in the same building, or one connected by telephone lines. The facilities of Internet make it possible for you to find computers which may have information of interest, access information and run programs on remote computers, also to copy files from remote computers into your own.

World Wide Web

Using the World Wide Web you view pages of information from remote computers. Some words, usually underlined on the screen, have links to other pages, which may be on other computers anywhere in the world. Each page has an address, a Uniform Resource Locator or URL, and also has a descriptive title. You can find a page by searching for a topic, and selecting one from the list of titles found. Alternatively you can type the URL address, if you know it. Once you have one page you can select an associated page by moving the pointer to an underlined word, and clicking with the mouse. Some sites have guides to genealogy on the Web, with thousands of links - see page 18.

The pages display text and graphics. Generally clicking on a link displays another page, but it can also start a sound or video recording, run a program, copy a file to your computer, or start a search. The World Wide Web is increasingly being used to do things which formerly required separate facilities.

Copying files (FTP)

Files on remote computers available for copying into your own include shareware genealogy packages, and lists of surname interests of individual researchers. The most general facility for copying files to (or from) your own computer is **ftp** (file transfer protocol), there are various simpler methods as well (see page 12).

Running programs (Telnet)

Some computers, for example library catalogue systems, have on-line search available, but programs quite different from those common on Internet. The facility **Telnet** makes your computer act as a terminal to a remote computer system. Use of this is decreasing, as more programs can be built into Web pages and Web sites. If you do encounter it, when you enter the system make a note of the keystrokes needed to leave it again.

Finding information of interest

There are special information pages and search programs to help you find information on the Internet - see page 17 for an example.

Finding surname interests

There are collections of pedigrees and collections of surname interests on Internet, available for search. It is also possible to search archives of messages seeking information about people of a particular surname. See page 19 for a description.

What you cannot do - yet

Many transcripts and indexes of UK records are not available for search on Internet. For example, the International Genealogical Index (IGI) and Ancestral File of the Church of Jesus Christ of Latter Day Saints are not on Internet; they are freely available on computer at Family History Centres of that Church, holding around two hundred million baptisms, marriages, etc. Many family history societies and individuals have compiled indexes of marriages, census entries, and a variety of other records. These may be published as booklets or microfiche, or there may be a search service available for a fee. A transcript and index of the 1881 census of the UK is being published on microfiche and CDROM, the result of a major collaborative project involving family history societies, the LDS church, and record offices. So you cannot do all your genealogy on the Web. But there are major indexes available for search on the Web - for example Commonwealth War Graves at **www.cwgc.org/**, Scottish Civil Registers, census and Parochial Records at **www.origins.net/GRO/**. No doubt the volume of transcripts and indexes will increase, so it is always worth searching to see what is available in your area of interest. For example see **http://homepages.enterprise.net/pjoiner/genuki/DUR/** where there are many parish registers for Durham.

WHAT YOU NEED FOR INTERNET

What you need to use Internet is a **computer**, a **telephone** line, and a subscription to a service from an **Internet Provider**. This is an organisation with its own computer system, telephone lines you can dial to connect your computer to theirs, and access to a network of faster communications links to other computers around the world. The connection from your computer goes from a **modem** which converts digital computer signals to sound signals which can be transmitted along the telephone line. The modem may be built in to the computer, or connected externally to its **serial port** socket. In your computer you need **communications software**, which looks after dialling, control of signals, detection and correction of errors. For a laptop or home desktop computer the communications software generally comes with the operating system, for example as part of Microsoft Windows. You also need **access software** which gives screens for you to view Web pages, type messages, read and reply to incoming messages, keep an address book, collect a group of related messages from a remote computer so you can read them off line without telephone charges, and use other Internet facilities. In most cases the access software is supplied by the Internet Provider, who has extra programs and helpful information in the central computer to support the various modes of access. For using the World Wide Web the main piece of software is the **browser**. When buying a new computer you will often find a browser, an email program, and a trial subscription to an Internet Provider included. There are beginning to be many ways of obtaining CDROM disks with free trial or even free continuing use of an Internet service, and all the software needed. These are generally easy to install, they search your computer for the modem connection and communications software. The only warning is that they may behave like cuckoos in the nest, replacing links to other Internet programs already in your computer.

As well as the access software supplied initially by the Internet provider, you may find later that you want additional or different programs known as "**client programs**" to use particular facilities. The concept behind this nomenclature is that the users are **clients**, and the central computers are **hosts** or **servers**.

Some Internet Providers have their own **on-line service**, with discussion groups, information services, shopping services, all available from the computer system of the provider, without needing links to other parts of the Internet. CompuServe is an example; it has particularly good forums for genealogy and for support of genealogy packages, with information from suppliers. These on-line services developed separately, they are now being integrated into the wider Internet.

Internet changes so fast that you will probably have to look at newspapers and magazines to get up to date information. There are two books which I bought and found useful: "Internet for Dummies" by John Levine & Carol Baroudi (IDG Books, California); "The Internet & World Wide Web - the Rough Guide" by Angus J Kennedy, distributed by Penguin Books.

There are frequent articles or news items about the use of Internet for Genealogy (and other aspects of the use of computers for genealogy) in the following magazines;
Family Tree Magazine, monthly, see title page of this book.
Computers in Genealogy, quarterly from Society of Genealogists, 14 Charterhouse Buildings, London EC1M 7BA; phone 0171 251 8799. Web address **www.sog.org.uk**
Genealogical Computing, quarterly from Ancestry Publishing, PO Box 476, Salt Lake City, Utah 84110, USA; phone 801 531 1790. Web address **www.ancestry.com**

When you are on-line you may obtain similar information from the *Journal of Online Genealogy* on the Web at **www.onlinegenealogy.com**, and from *Eastman's Online Genealogy Newsletter* which is sent weekly by email free of charge - back issues at **www.ancestry.com/columns/eastman/index.htm** have instructions for subscribing.

EMAIL - PRIVATE MESSAGES

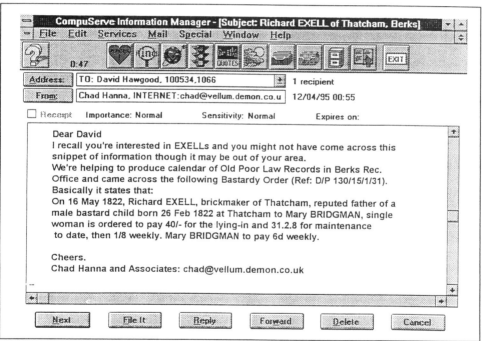

Figure 1 - email

Email is sent directly from one person to another known person. In the example Chad Hanna knew I was interested in the Excell surname and variants. He happened to come across a document mentioning an Exell, and sent me an email with the details.

An email has a subject - here it is "Richard EXELL of Thatcham, Berks" which appears at the top of the screen. The name and email addresses of sender and recipient are shown. (The form of these addresses varies slightly depending whether both parties use the same on-line service.) In practice I rarely type an address - when I receive a message I can make an automatic transfer of the details to the **address book** in my computer.

When I am looking at the message I am not using the telephone - I connect, ask for all messages to be transferred to my computer, they appear in the "in basket" of my computer, and I disconnect to save phone charges. What makes email so convenient is the ease of answering. Just click on the "reply" box at the bottom of the screen, and a blank message screen opens, addressed to the person who sent the message, and with the same subject - you can just type a quick reply. Email programs also make it easy to copy text from the incoming message into the reply, marked with > and < angle brackets - but don't overdo this, copy the relevant question rather than the whole message. Normally I put the replies in the "out basket", and send them all in one go. It typically takes about fifteen seconds connected to send a few replies, or to collect a few incoming messages.

Various areas of the computers mentioned in the last paragraph are directories. In Figure 1, the CompuServe Information Manager screen, each is represented by an icon in the tool-bar near the top of the screen. Move the pointer to the "in tray" icon and click the mouse, the screen displays a list of the messages received, with subjects and names of senders. Click on a particular one to read it. Click on the "File it" button at the bottom of the screen, it is moved from the in tray directory to one of the filing cabinet directories. Later you can click on the filing cabinet icon at the top of the screen, and display again any message previously filed. Click on the "address book" icon at the top of the screen to add or edit an entry in the address book. This is a list of names, email addresses, and an area for notes. The "in tray" and "out tray" icons change appearance from grey to black lines when there is mail waiting to be read or despatched.

Also convenient is the facility to "Forward" the message to someone else. The original sender's name and address appear in the forwarded message as text, you can put in your own comments, and send it on to someone else. The other boxes at the bottom of the screen are just normal facilities as you get in a word processor - you can file the message, delete it, "cancel" to leave it unchanged where it is.

You can usually add a **signature** to your outgoing messages. This is a couple of lines of information about yourself - your email address, what city and country you live in, maybe the main surname you are researching. Keep it short.

Many people have email available at work or college, and can use it for private messages, even if they cannot use a computer for other Internet access. Increasingly people will have computers with email at home. It is a very good way of keeping in touch with the family, and has the advantage that people do tend to make a reply very quickly.

In its simplest form a message can only contain 7-bit ASCII data, which means that accented letters, currency symbols and graphics cannot be transferred. The characters generally available are shown in the next three lines, (32 per line, in groups of 8) in order of their ASCII codes from 32 which is a space to 127 which is a tilde. You may be able to type other characters, but they may get changed when displayed on another computer.

```
  ! " # $ % & '   ( ) * + , - . /   0 1 2 3 4 5 6 7   8 9 : ; < = > /
@ A B C D E F G   H I J K L M N O   P Q R S T U V W   X Y Z [ \ ] ^ _
` a b c d e f g   h i j k l m n o   p q r s t u v w   x y z { | } ~
```

One notable omission from the list above is the pound sign, £. Although there is provision for national character sets, with the pound £ and hash (number) # being swapped in a UK set, you will usually find the above set in use.

There are several ways of sending 8-bit data with extra characters. Within many mailing systems you can **attach** a file to a text message. More generally a file of 8-bit data can be converted to 7-bit; you will see references to programs called **uuencode** and **MIME**. These perform compression as well as encoding 8-bit characters. The receiving system then regenerates the 8-bit file. Most mailing systems perform the encode and decode automatically, but you may encounter an encoded message, and may see references in the header of a message. For example one of my messages to a mailing list was returned to me in a reply and included the statement:

X-MIME-Autoconverted: from quoted-printable to 8bit by bl-30.rootsweb.com

If you have a coding problem ask the sender to retransmit the message as plain text.

WEB-BASED EMAIL AND PERMANENT EMAIL ADDRESSES

An email address is normally of the form yourname@your-internet-provider. For example mine is David_Hawgood@Compuserve.com, and I have an account with Compuserve. But this is inconvenient in a couple of ways. One is that people often change their Internet provider, and would like to keep their email address. The other is that you may want an email address when you have not actually got an email account, or travel and use computers in Internet cafés. Both of these are catered for. For the first, you have an Internet email address but have a forwarding arrangement, rather like a Post Office Box number or accommodation address. One comes from Bigfoot with a web site at **www.bigfoot.com**. Through this I could register an email address JohnDoe@bigfoot.com and mail would be forwarded to my real email address. The second type of service comes from web-based email services. You access a web site and register a name and password. Then you can send and receive emails by accessing a web page through a browser. One example is hotmail, at web site **http://hotmail.msn.co.uk**. Both of these are free - they display advertising on the website or add a short advertising message to emails to pay for the service. There are great changes in progress on this type of service, look at magazines for news.

LOOKUP EXCHANGE AND SURNAME LISTS

At first you may think you have few friends with email, so it will be difficult to have a useful discussion. Once you start including your email address with your postal address, you will find messages start to arrive. Add it to your Christmas card, you might be surprised to receive chatty messages from nephews and god-children. There are also ways of obtaining email addresses of individuals. I describe ways of finding other people researching the same surname, also ways of finding people by name, starting at page 19. For most counties there are surname lists with email addresses of researchers - to find them start from the structured lists of counties on the Web in GENUKI **www.genuki.org.uk** and in Cyndi's list at **www.cyndislist.com/** (there are other helpful sites listing genealogy information, see page 18). There are also lists of people who own reference books and are prepared to look up entries for people who enquire by email. For details see **www.geocities.com/Heartland/Plains/8555/lookup.html**. They may even visit a library and look up a reference - there is a lot of mutual help among genealogists on the Internet. And don't forget it is an exchange - what can you contribute?

CONFERENCES - PUBLIC MESSAGES

MAILING LISTS

Mailing lists are described in this section, newsgroups in the next one. Both are ways in which you can read messages from a group of people interested in a particular subject. The essential difference is that with a mailing list, if you subscribe to the list, then all messages about that subject get sent to your computer. Messages in some mailing lists are archived, available for searching. With a newsgroup, the messages are stored on one or more central computers, and you browse through recent ones as you want.

Either way, you can reply to a message. You can either make a public reply, posted with the original and connected to it in a "**thread**", or you can reply to the originator only. There is "**netiquette**" about messages - DON'T SHOUT, i.e. don't use all capitals. Don't clutter up the public area with replies of interest only to one recipient. Keep your message short, and only copy very small salient parts of the message you are replying to. Often there is a document with **Frequently Asked Questions (FAQs)** and their answers - read it, and don't ask those questions again. You should not include attachments with messages to mailing lists. But don't be afraid to ask a question - it's just like asking a question of a colleague at the next desk in an office.

The GENBRIT mailing list is linked to the soc.genealogy.britain newsgroup. GENBRIT is in fact four mailing lists:
GENBRIT-L which sends each posting as an individual message.
GENBRIT-D which sends each posting as a MIME encoded digest. This will contain a number of postings collected together into a single message.
GENBRIT-NMD which send the digests in a non MIME encoded format.
GENBRIT-I which sends just a list of the messages in each digest. It includes directions on how to retrieve the messages you are interested in.

To subscribe to the mailing list and to get individual messages, write to GENBRIT-L-request@rootsweb.com, and in the body of the message (not the subject line) say: SUBSCRIBE

Do not put anything else in the message. Remove any 'signature' lines or the server may get confused. If you want to subscribe to any of the other lists, replace the GENBRIT-L in the address with the list name you wish to join. For example, to join the digest list, use the address GENBRIT-D-request@rootsweb.com.

TO LEAVE THE LIST
Write to GENBRIT-L-request@rootsweb.com, and in the body of the message (not the subject line) say: UNSUBSCRIBE

Figure 2 GENBRIT-L mailing list - extracts from subscription information

GENBRIT is a mailing list for British Genealogy. You join the mailing list, and messages are then sent directly to your own computer, just as if they were messages sent for you alone. But the message is sent at the same time to anyone else who has joined (subscribed to) that mailing list. You can leave a list at any time, to stop the flow of messages. The messages are all archived, so you can search old subjects and retrieve ones of interest.

Figure 2 contains extracts from the information message sent when you subscribe. Because there can be large numbers of messages, there are options to help you view only those of interest. One is to subscribe to the digest, which sends one email containing a

```
Subject: genuki-digest 238, dated 12 Dec 95

Contents

Article#9465 - Subject: Lourigan-surname?
Article#9466 - Subject: LOCKEY, Lancashire and Durham c.1838-1880's
Article#9467 - Subject: Re: Correct Pronunciation of REGAN
Article#9468 - Subject: BARRITT, Little Lever, Lancashire c.1880's
Article#9469 - Subject: Re: Stanton: who knows about this surname?
Article#9470 - Subject: DALEY
Article#9471 - Subject: Re: HAILEY...Scottish or Irish?..
```

Figure 3 Digest of messages in Genuki-L mailing list

```
----- Start of Article -----
Article#9466 - Subject: LOCKEY, Lancashire and Durham c.1838-1880's
From: blackburn@hunterlink.net.au (Norma Blackburn)

I'm interested in hearing from anyone who might have information on the following:
   Samual LOCKEY, born around 1838 in Sedgefield Durham, he married a woman called
Hannah from Little Lever, Lancashire, where he moved to. They had 2 children that I
know of. He died possibly in 1908 in the Bolton district.His children were;
Alice LOCKEY, born c. 1897 she married William FLETCHER and had children from
1885.
Samual LOCKEY, born around 1874.

Norma Blackburn
New South Wales
Australia
blackburn@hunterlink.net.au
```

Figure 4 Detail of a message in Genuki-L mailing list

number of messages or "articles" - often one email per day. Another option on lists like GENBRIT with high volume is to receive only a list of subjects, not the text of the messages; there are instructions for retrieving individual messages of interest. For GENBRIT there is also an option to receive messages without the MIME encoding and decoding mentioned above. When you subscribe to a list make a point of keeping the first message you receive - it tells you how to leave the list later. The message also tells you how to get the FAQ (Frequently Asked Questions) file, and gives guidance on the subjects which are welcome - it suggests GENNAM for surname queries, GENMTD about methods, GENCMP about genealogical computing.

The examples in Figures 3 and 4 are from the GENUKI list which was a predecessor of GENBRIT (it included Ireland, which now has its own list). A digest starts with a list of articles, with numbers, as shown in Figure 3. The digest continues with the text of the day's messages. Figure 4 is a typical message, asking for information about a particular Samual Lockey. Other messages have lists of occurrences of one surname, or announce the existence of a database of some particular place or surname. Letters to *Family Tree Magazine* show that some readers have found unknown relatives through the mailing lists, but far more have been able to add to their one name studies, and get in touch with other people pursuing studies on the same name in different parts of the world.

The message to subscribe is an email sent to an automatic message handler, a server. The address is that of the server. The names of the servers are pieces of software; you may encounter listproc, listserv, majordomo and others. For some you put commands like "subscribe" or "help" as the subject of the message, for others they go in the message text - if in doubt send a message with "help" in both. To find the address of a list you have to use some sort of searcher or guide - see the guides listed on page 18, for example.

You will often find that messages in a mailing list are "echoed" (copied) to a newsgroup; for example the newsgroup soc.genealogy.britain receives a copy of messages to the GENBRIT mailing list. This gives two alternative ways of seeing the messages. Addresses, descriptions and instructions for joining mailing lists are given on several World Wide Web sites - see GENUKI on **www.genuki.org.uk** or John Fuller's pages at **http://members.aol.com/johnf14246/gen_mail.html**.

You can also search message digests by content. There is an example of searching message archives for surnames on page 22.

USENET OR NEWSGROUPS

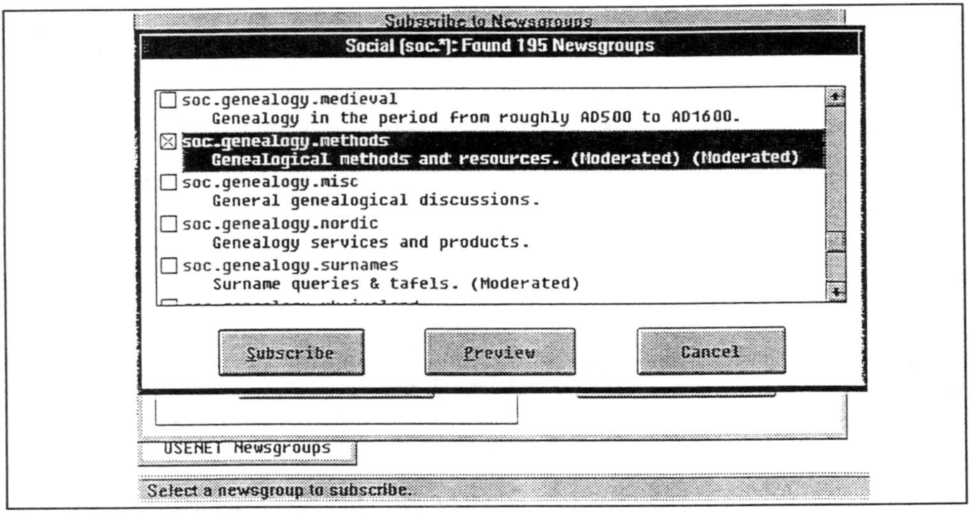

Figure 5 Selecting a newsgroup

As described above, in a mailing list messages about a particular subject are copied to the computers of individual subscribers. In a newsgroup the messages are sent to many network computers. To read them you connect, browse through a list of subjects, then either mark the ones of interest to be sent to your own computer, or read them while connected. The newsgroup system is also called **Usenet**, the name of the network of computers on which the organisation developed.

The first time I went into newsgroups from CompuServe I was shown some screens of information about newsgroups, how they work, and the "netiquette" of using them. Then I went through a hierarchy of screens. CompuServe was taking 195 newsgroups in

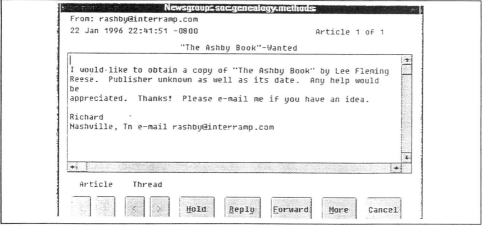

Thread	Articles
"The Ashby Book"-Wanted	1
?Care and preservcat	1
Attn: All Genealogical Societies	1
Ben Franklin's wife's mothers maiden name	1
BURKE'S, DeBRETT's, COKAYNE - Accurate?	3
CDs as research tool	1
Civil War Records	1
HELP NEEDED FROM CHICAGO,IL	1

As is
Quoted
Decoded

Retrieve   Get   Clear   Create

Mark   Retrieve Marked   Cancel

Figure 6 Newsgroup - subjects of messages

the "social" category which includes genealogy. From the list of newsgroups in Figure 5 I chose to preview "soc.genealogy.methods" which meant I could read the messages, but not send my own. Figure 6 is a list of topics. A "thread" is a group of messages all on one topic. Some newsgroups encourage readers to reply to the whole newsgroup, so that the message is added to the thread. Others prefer most responses to be sent direct to the initiator of the message.

Newsgroup: soc.genealogy.methods

From: rashby@interramp.com
22 Jan 1996 22:41:51 -0800   Article 1 of 1

                    "The Ashby Book"-Wanted

I would like to obtain a copy of "The Ashby Book" by Lee Fleming Reese. Publisher unknown as well as its date. Any help would be appreciated. Thanks! Please e-mail me if you have an idea.

Richard
Nashville, Tn e-mail rashby@interramp.com

Article   Thread

Hold   Reply   Forward   More   Cancel

Figure 7 Newsgroup - viewing a complete message

I chose to retrieve the topic **"The Ashby Book" - Wanted**. Figure 7 shows the message displayed, from Richard Ashby in Nashville, Tennessee wanting to obtain a copy of a particular book. Incidentally, when I contacted him for permission to reproduce his message, he told me he found the book as a result of posting his message. Boxes at the bottom of the screen allow you to reply, forward the message to someone else, move to another article in the same thread, or move to another thread - ie another topic. These boxes at the bottom come from the particular software supplied by CompuServe, other software gives similar facilities in different ways. Many of them are **off-line readers**; on some you download the list of topics, look at it offline, then retrieve the ones of interest. I can do this with the CompuServe system, I just disconnect to save phone charges once I am displaying the list, then it reconnects when I ask for a particular message. Some off-line readers can perform quite complex selections of messages to down-load.

INTERNET RELAY CHAT - TYPED CONVERSATION

With the email and conference facilities described so far, you type a message, send it, disconnect, then reconnect after several hours or next day to look for replies. With Internet Relay Chat a group of people all connect to the Internet and stay connected while they type messages and receive answers, they communicate live on-line. You need a special program to do this, one is mIRC. You can download it from the Web at **www.mirc.co.uk**, where there is also a description of the system. Install the program, choose an Undernet server from "setup information", type **/join #genealogy** in the status window. There are also Internet Relay Chat sessions in the International Internet Genealogical Society - that is on the Web at **www.iigs.org/index.htm.en** with details of IRC at **www.iigs.org/irc/index.htm.en**.

COPYING FILES - FTP

If you want to send a file from your computer to someone else, it is usually easiest to include it in an email message, or attach it to an email message. If the files only contain text, the characters included in the table of 7-bit ASCII characters shown on page 6, they can be sent with no conversion. Otherwise they may have to be encoded; usually this is done automatically by the mailing system, but you might have to agree with the recipient which coding system to use, **uuencode** and MIME are common. It is also common practice to compress files before encoding them. The most common system for compression is **zip**. Programs **pkzip** and **winzip** to perform this are both shareware, respectively for IBM-compatible computers with DOS and Windows. You may find that a zip decompression program is already on your computer, or on the CDROM that came with it containing the operating system and utilities.

The most general facility for retrieving files is **file transfer protocol** or **ftp**. You will often see ftp addresses quoted when you are told where to get copies of files. Look up ftp in the help screens of your Internet system before starting to use it. You may have to type a fairly complicated command, or your system may make it easier for you. In practice most of the file transfers I have initiated have either been started from World Wide Web pages, or else have been obtained within CompuServe. In either case the transfer has been easy, and the file just gets copied into my system. It appears automatically in a nominated directory, one called "Download" on my system.

What files are available? Certainly shareware or demonstration copies of genealogy programs. There is a good selection of these held within CompuServe, for example. Also utility programs to perform functions like "zip" and "uuencode". You will also find files of surname interests - there is more about this in the section starting on page 19. Answers to "Frequently Asked Questions" from newsgroups are available - see page 9.

WORLD WIDE WEB

The World Wide Web gives you a way to look at pages of information stored by many different organisations. To start using the World Wide Web you enter an address, known as a **Uniform Resource Locator** or **URL**. The page with that address is sent to your computer. The first screenful is displayed - you can choose whether or not to have graphics images displayed as they take longer to load. The rest of the page is loaded into store in your computer.

The World Wide Web needs special access software, a browser. The two best known are Internet Explorer (from Microsoft) and Netscape. They provide facilities for sending and receiving email, reading newsgroups, also ftp and Telnet, so they provide a very large proportion of the Internet access you need within one package.

Figure 8 is made up from three parts of the "UK and Ireland" page of GENUKI, the UK and Ireland Genealogical Information Service. What is really clever in the World Wide Web is that it is not just displayed text and graphics, it is **hypertext**. Held with any underlined phrase is the URL of an appropriate web page. The URL for a Hypertext page starts with **http**, standing for "**HyperText Transfer Protocol**". The one for GENUKI is **http://www.genuki.org.uk/**. Most browsers will recognise anything starting www as being a Web address, so (as in this book) the http:// is often omitted - but for addresses not starting www it is needed. "**www.genuki.org.uk**" is the name of an Internet domain; using address **www.genuki.org.uk** or **www.genuki.org.uk/** (with a slash at the end) obtains the default home page for the domain. **www.genuki.org.uk/big/** obtains the default page for a directory "big" - (for British Isles Genealogy) within the domain. Continuing after the slash obtains a specific page, for example the main index to Genuki is **www.genuki.co.uk/mindex.html**. You will find that most end with .htm or .html to show they contain Hypertext Markup Language. If you find an address does not work, try shortening it back to the previous "/" (slash character); this may display a default page with a link to the one you want.

Click the mouse on the phrase, the system fetches that page. It may be on the same computer, it may be somewhere quite different. For example the third paragraph of Figure 8 includes ". . map showing the counties in England, Scotland and Wales ". Click on the underlined phrase, the map appears - part of it is shown in Figure 9. The underlined link words are also coloured, and the colour changes (e.g. from blue to red) on links you have accessed.

In the section of Figure 8 headed "Gazetteers" click on the underlined "online gazetteer". A form is displayed from the Ordnance Survey pages of the web, you fill in a place name of interest and it tells you the location - see Figure 10. Continuing with the examples, in the "Societies" section at the bottom of Figure 8, clicking on Society of Genealogists leads to a brochure, library guide with floor plans, and a bookshop catalogue with on-line ordering. Clicking on Federation of Family History Societies leads to a list of member societies, and again a bookshop catalogue, with order form. Other parts of GENUKI give information about record offices, for example with the text of a number of guidance leaflets from the Public Record Office.

You don't have to stay connected while you read the information. You can disconnect, and still browse up and down the current page, and even go back and forward among the other pages displayed recently. You can print out pages by using "Print" in the

Genuki home page | Contents

The UK and Ireland

The **UK and Ireland** are regarded, for the purposes of this Genealogical Information Service, as being made up of **England**, **Ireland** (i.e. *Northern Ireland* and the *Republic of Ireland*), **Wales**, and **Scotland**, together with the **Channel Islands** and the **Isle of Man**. Together, these constitute the *British Isles* - which is a geographical term for a group of islands lying off the north-west coast of mainland Europe. (Legally, the Channel Islands and the Isle of Man are largely self governing, and are not part of the United Kingdom.)

This page provides pointers to these six areas, plus information which relates to the UK and Ireland as a whole. The UK and Ireland is in fact divided into a large number of <u>Administrative Regions,</u> whose names are often abbreviated by genealogists using a set of three-letter "Chapman codes".

These codes are also given in a map showing the counties in <u>England, Scotland and Wales</u> prior to the re-organisation which took place in 1974. Riley Williams (KB8PPG@g7heaven.wintermute.co.uk) prepared it originally, with modifications by Mike Fisher. The corresponding one for <u>Ireland</u> has been produced by Brian Randell based on a map obtained from Paddy Waldron.

Gazetteers

The Ordnance Survey has made available an <u>online gazetteer</u> which provides means of searching a large list of placenames extracted from the Ordnance Survey database - but not individual farms and houses. The search will return the name of the place, its County, an Ordnance Survey grid reference and the number of the 1:50 000 Landranger series map that the place appears on.

Genealogy

A number of general <u>guides and textbooks</u> on genealogy and family history within the UK and Ireland have been recommended by various readers of the soc.genealogy.uk+ireland newsgroup. In addition books relating to particular regions and topics will be found listed on the appropriate pages, and at the relevant headings, elsewhere in this information service.

Societies

There is a major national society, <u>The Society of Genealogists</u>, a large number of local societies grouped together into the <u>Federation of Family History Societies</u>, and other societies that cater for genealogy, family history and associated interests. There are <u>details about the societies</u> and contact addresses, and some individual societies have their own pages giving further information.

Figure 8 GENUKI - URL http://www.genuki.org.uk/

File menu - they come out nicely formatted. Later, you can click on one of the links, the system asks "Do you want to reconnect" and you resume from that point, connecting to Internet and loading a new page. When I started using the World Wide Web I did not realise I could do this disconnection and reconnection. My first few sessions using the Web were 20 minute phone calls as I linked and viewed and printed. Now some sessions are between one and two minutes - retrieve a page, follow a link, probably follow a further link, then disconnect to read the information obtained. To balance this, unfortunately some pages take an age to load, particularly at busy times like late evening in the UK when people in both America and Europe are on line.

GENUKI is structured on locality levels, so there is some information for the whole of UK and Ireland, then for each individual county, then for some individual towns and parishes. At each locality level there can be information about church records, history, archives, societies, etc. This structure is based on the catalogue of the Family History Library of the LDS Church (incidentally, that LDS catalogue is available on CD-ROM at their Family History Centres, but is not yet on Internet). In some cases there are links from GENUKI to Web pages for individual Family History Societies, for all societies there is at least the postal address of the secretary.

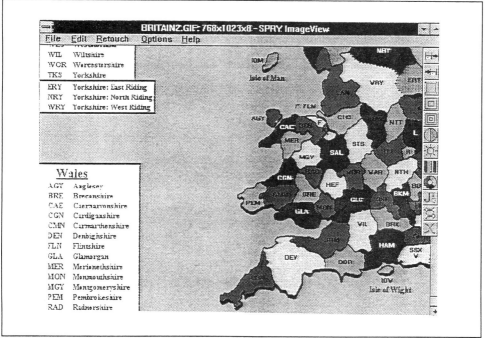

Figure 9 - Map obtained by clicking the mouse on a link in the GENUKI page

Figure 9 is the map obtained by clicking on <u>England, Scotland and Wales</u> in Figure 8. The map is transmitted as a condensed image file, and expanded by viewing software. I saved the image in Windows bitmap format, and later viewed and printed it with Windows Paintbrush. This map display is an example of retrieving a complete file from a remote computer and copying it into your own computer. Here the retrieval is performed by the World Wide Web software. I downloaded this when preparing the first edition of the book, and the particular file format was viewed with Spry Image View. This is an example of a "plug-in" program - you may find that if you download some sound or video or even a word-processor document your browser will start up the appropriate application from your system that can play or display the file - or you might get a message to say that no viewer is available for the particular file format.

Ordnance Survey - Gazetteer Search Results

Here are the results of your search for "Thatcham". You might like to look at the <u>Landranger series sheet coverage of the UK</u> to see where these places are.

Name	County	Grid Ref	Landranger sheet
Thatcham	Berks	SU5167	174

You can search the database again by filling in the box below and clicking the Search button.

<u>Return to Ordnance Survey main menu</u>

Figure 10 - Gazetteer

Figure 10 shows the result of a remote search of an Ordnance Survey gazetteer. I typed in "Thatcham", and clicked on the search button. My search request was passed back to the Ordnance Survey computer, which ran a search program, and passed the results back to my computer. In this case there was just one match, the Thatcham in Berkshire mentioned in the email message in Figure 1. The answer gave me the county, the Ordnance Survey grid reference to the nearest kilometre, and the number of the 1:50,000 scale map on which Thatcham appears. I also tried "Aston" which gave me a full page of places called or starting with "Aston".

This search of a database is a simple example of running a program on a remote computer. You don't get the full Ordnance Survey database of places in your computer, just the ones which match your enquiry.

LIBRARIES, ARCHIVES AND MUSEUMS ON THE WEB

Many libraries, archives and museums have web sites. You can find them from structured information systems on the Web like GENUKI, or by searching as described in the next section. Here I will give references to a few.

The British Library is at **www.bl.uk/** with its on-line catalogue OPAC 97 at **http://opac97.bl.uk/** (OPAC stands for Online Public Access Catalogue). COPAC: University Research Library Catalogue is at **http://copac.ac.uk/copac/**. For public libraries see EARL: Familia. Resources of Public Libraries in Britain and Ireland for family history research at **www.earl.org.uk/familia/index.html**, and for libraries in

London see **http://pitcairn.lib.uci.edu/largo/largo/largo.html** which is LARGO: Libraries and Archives Research Guide Online - London.

The Royal Commission on Historical Manuscripts is at **www.hmc.gov.uk/main.htm**. This is far more useful than you might expect - you can search for subjects, places and names in the titles of document collections in many archives in Britain. The Public Record Office in London is at **www.pro.gov.uk/** - the text of many information leaflets is available, an on-line bookshop, a great variety of helpful information. The General Register Office for Scotland is at **www.open.gov.uk/gros/groshome.htm** - within that there is a link to Scots Origins giving searches of vital record, census and Old Parochial Register indexes, for a fee currently £6 for a day.

Many museums have web sites - for those specialising in military history try **http://chide.museum.org.uk/military.index.html** which is The Military Collections, Museums & Sites of Interest Directory.

SEARCHING FOR INFORMATION

Yahoo Search Results

Found 3 matches containing **family history library** . Displaying matches 1-3.

Arts:Humanities:**History** :Genealogy:Organizations
- Ellen Payne Odom Genealogy **Library** - The EPO **library** houses genealogical reference materials, including holdings of 80 Scottish Clans. They offer a free (US only) 'snail mail' publication: 'The **Family** Tree.'

Regional:Countries:Ireland:Culture:**History** :Genealogy
- UK & Ireland Genealogical Information Service - This server is a virtual **library** of material relating to genealogy and **family history** of the British Isles.

Regional:Countries:United Kingdom: **History**
- UK & Ireland Genealogical Information Service - This server is a virtual **library** of material relating to genealogy and **family history** of the British Isles.

Other Search Engines
Open Text | Alta Vista | Lycos | WebCrawler | Inktomi | DejaNews | More...

Figure 11 Yahoo finding matches on Internet for "Family" & "History" & "Library"

When I was obtaining the GENUKI page shown in Figure 8, I already knew the Universal Resource Locator of the front page of GENUKI as it had been published in *Family Tree Magazine* and *Computers in Genealogy* (in articles which are now on-line within GENUKI).

Once I had the GENUKI page I was able to find the Ordnance Survey gazetteer just by clicking on links displayed on screen, and I saved some of those into my "favourites" so in future they appeared on menus at the top of my screen. But how do you find your way around the World Wide Web if you have no convenient start point? The answer is to use a **"search engine"** which looks around the Web. On the CompuServe Home Page which appeared when I first started using the Web in 1995 I found a choice called *Search Wizard*. This turned out to be a link to a search engine called *Yahoo* at **www.yahoo.com/**.

This builds a searchable structured list of sites, grouped into categories. First I searched for "genealogy". This gave a list of 165 sites, presented 25 at a time. This was an extremely useful list, with all sorts of services I did not know about before, or had not tried - for example *The Green Pages* of Irish-related Internet resources including genealogy.

I also tried searching for **family history library**. I set the search in *Yahoo* to look for entries in which all three words appeared. This found three matches, shown in Figure 11. If you click on the underlined part of an entry, you activate a link and load the home page of the relevant service - very convenient, and often quicker than typing the URL even if you know it. In this case two of the entries were the same, the GENUKI information. It found one via Ireland and one via the UK in a structured list. The third entry, the Ellen Payne Odom Genealogy Library, I had not heard of before. In 1995 there were three hits, in 1999 there were 55 - and they included addresses of Family History Centres of the LDS Church, which were missing before.

The Yahoo search shown in Figure 11 also shows the links to other search engines. I find I use **Yahoo** for its search of sites within a hierarchical structure, and Alta Vista at **www.altavista.com** because it searches and indexes text within Web pages. If you read newspaper and magazine articles about Internet you will often find descriptions of ways of finding information on the Web. This is the best way to find out the features of the various search facilities - they keep changing. Because the Internet is so unstructured with thousands of independent computers, searching for information gets a lot of attention.

The growth of the Web means there is more to find, but you have to know how to make the search precise. A Yahoo search for genealogy which found 165 sites in 1995 now finds over 2800. Alta Vista searches find even more. On most search engines you can put a + sign before a word to specify that it must be present, and a - sign to say it must not be included. Other general facilities are that an uppercase letter in the enquiry finds only upper case, lower case finds upper or lower case. And you can use wild cards - "genealog*" finds genealogy and genealogical. If I search for Hawgood I get 1500 hits in Alta Vista - many are references to American hockey player Greg Hawgood, eg "Sharks defenseman Hawgood suspended". +Hawgood -hockey reduces the number of hits to 600. I noticed a firm in "Hawgood Street, London E3" and a search on +Hawgood +Street found others. In fact enclosing this in quotes "Hawgood Street" would probably have been even better. Look at the help screens in the search engine you like, try some other search engines to see how they vary. And when you publish your own family history pages, include the word "genealogy" in the title of the page - a search for a particular surname and "genealogy" is probably the one most people try.

When you look at the "page" obtained by a search, you may not see the words you wanted - a web page can be tens or hundreds of printed pages. But the browser has word finding facilities like those of a word processor, to search within the page which has been loaded. On Internet Explorer key Control and F, or choose the Edit menu, then Find.

There are some useful guides to genealogy on the Internet with thousands of links. For example:

www.cyndislist.com/ - Cyndi's List
www.gengateway.com/ - Genealogy Gateway To The Web by Steve Lacy
www.familytreemaker.com/links/index.html - Family Tree Maker Genealogy SiteFinder

PUBLISH YOUR OWN WEB PAGES

Many Internet Providers give each subscriber an allocation of space for World Wide Web pages. These are held on central computers, so they are available whether or not your own computer is connected. For the genealogist, this means that you can publish your pedigree on Internet. You can arrange that there is a link from the main people in a pedigree to information pages about them, or pictures. You can also put in links to maps of their area. You can also provide links to pages belonging to other people or organisations - for example those of Family History Societies of which you are a member.

The first pages I put on the Web were prepared using the CompuServe "Home Page Wizard". It gets you to fill in a form about your self, your occupation and hobbies. It prepares an introductory page from this. You can then edit it, add more text, add external links, add extra pages. I don't pretend the result is as sophisticated as other home pages I have seen, but I was able to prepare and publish some pages without any knowledge of the "HyperText Markup Language" which is used to specify Web pages. My next set were parts of my family history, prepared from within the genealogy package *Family Origins* and were placed on a site belonging to the publisher of the package. Within a couple of days of submitting them I received an enquiry by email by someone who had searched the Web for "Hawgood" - showing it is better to shout than listen. To go with the second edition of this book I am preparing pages using Microsoft FrontPage Express, which came with the browser Internet Explorer. Whatever Internet Provider you use, you will find programs available for preparing your own Web pages. I publish a book *Web Publishing for Genealogy* by Peter Christian (available from Family Tree Magazine - address on title page). To go with this there is a Web site with more information, and links to providers of special software for publishing genealogical information on the Web: see **www.walrus.dircon.co.uk/wpg/**

FINDING SURNAME INTERESTS

How do you locate other family historians interested in people of your surname? There are a number of surname search services on Internet. These services will develop rapidly, and it is well worth submitting your own surname interests - you are very likely to get in touch with someone else researching the same surname, and I have heard of a number of people who have discovered distant cousins through the Internet.

When searching for surnames, categories of information you may find include:
- Location and date range, with contact details of the interested genealogist
- Pedigree containing the name, with events and other linked persons
- Queries about the name
- Links to web pages containing genealogies for the name
- Transcripts and indexes systematically extracted from original records

INFORMATION FORMATS FOR GENEALOGY

There are special formats for submitting surname interests:

Roots Surname List uses its own format to show dates and places of interest.

GENDEX uses its own format to construct an index to the submitter's web pages.

GEDCOM used by GenServ and others, is a standard file format for transferring lineage-linked family information. For each person GEDCOM can include name, sex, title, date and place of birth and death, and much more. It can also hold links to children, and links to spouses, with marriage date and place. Most genealogy packages can generate or accept GEDCOM data.

Tiny Tafels are now used mainly on personal Web pages. A Tiny Tafel is a short and formal statement of the surname interests of a researcher, organised for easy handling by computers. The format starts with the name, address, and phone number of the submitter, and ends with the date generated. The body is a set of lines like:
B422 1799*1906:BLACKMORE\Wraxall Somerset ENG/Melbourne Victoria AUS
This starts with the Soundex code B422 for the surname. 1799 is the year of the first Blackmore event in my database, 1906 the last; Wraxall and Melbourne are the corresponding places. The asterisk shows high interest in the first person, the colon shows moderate interest in the Blackmore who died in Melbourne (my wife's great-grandmother), and a full stop would show slight interest, a space would show no interest. Tiny Tafels have been used on Fidonet, a network of Bulletin Boards. With the growth of the World Wide Web, use of Bulletin Boards has decreased. Tiny Tafels are generated automatically by a number of genealogy packages, for example Brother's Keeper.

Before you prepare a submission in any format, obtain and read the text files which explain it. Reading them, it is clear that the organisers receive a lot of submissions from people who have not read the documentation.

SURNAME SEARCH SERVICES

Roots Surname List (RSL) at **http://searches.rootsweb.com/cgi-bin/Genea/rsl**
Each line of a submission to this list is a surname, the first and last dates at which the researcher has information, and a series of places to which the family moved. As an example I searched for "Blackmore" and found 31 entries, of which one was:
Blackmore 1612 1694 ENG > MA, USA drlutz
This says that the researcher whose code is "drlutz" has details of a Blackmore family in England in 1612, which moved to Maryland, USA, and there are further records up to 1694. A line can include more than two place names, but the total line cannot exceed 80 characters. Searching from the World Wide Web, I just clicked on the code to get the name, email and postal addresses of the submitter. It is also possible to register and have later additions emailed to you. Searches are free, searchers are encouraged to sponsor Rootsweb.

GENSERV at **www.genserv.com/**
GenServ is a database of GEDCOM files. In January 1999 it had 15 million individuals in 12000 GEDCOM files. You can get further details and make one search free of charge through the World Wide Web . This one free trial gives forenames and dates of people in the GEDCOM files matching your request. You can also make free searches to find out how many people with a surname occur - I found 422 Blackmore, and 6 Hawgood. To participate further you have to submit a GEDCOM file yourself; you can prepare this from your own family information in most genealogy packages. To participate in the system you must give an email address at which you can receive messages. It does not have to be your own email address, that of a friend will do fine, so long as messages will

be given to you. Once you have submitted a GEDCOM file to GenServ (by email, ftp, through the Web, or by ordinary post) you can do detailed searches, providing descendant and ancestor and source note information. You can also get details of people in other GEDCOM files who might be the same as people in your files, allowing for missing first names, likely mis-spellings, and approximate dates. It is thus more than a surname list, it can contain linked pedigrees with source notes, and becomes one way to publish your own pedigree. You then get a free two-month subscription, and can extend it for £8 per annum.

GENDEX at www.gendex.com/gendex/

Gendex indexes genealogy data held elsewhere on the Web. The scheme is that anyone with a Web site can send an index to their site in a special index - information about generating their index is on their Web site, the format is beginning to be available within genealogy packages. In January 1999 there are 10 million individuals with 300,000 surnames in 2700 databases. I found 127 Blackmore entries, and searching for Hawgood found: Hannah /Hawgood/ BEF 1715 Orlingbury, Northamptonshire
This entry has a link to a Web site with the pedigree in which Hannah Hawgood appears.

GenWeb at www.worldgenweb.org/

The GenWeb project started with people in the USA finding that all the information on the Web was either queries or pedigrees, little systematic extraction and indexing of original documents. They started doing transcripts and posting them on the Web. Volunteers coordinate activities on a county-by-county basis, often with an associated mailing list. The lists, transcripts and search programs are hosted on the Rootsweb site. The structure has been extended World Wide, and includes links to family history societies, archives, etc. For some countries there is **GenConnect** on which users can post queries, biographies, obituaries, wills, family bible entries, etc. A complicated site, much variation in coverage from place to place, well worth a look.

Kindred Connections at www.kindredkonnections.com/

This site claims to index 87 million names. It is a combination of submitted pedigrees and transcripts. You can get a free hour of use by transcribing a record displayed in facsimile on the screen, and a free month by submitting a GEDCOM file.

Ancestry at www.ancestry.com/main.htm

Ancestry has a great variety of databases, and sometimes has special offers for searches.

I Found it! at www.gensource.com/

"I Found it!" searches Internet sites for genealogy

Broderbund at www.familytreemaker.com/index.html
Excite at www.excite.com/lifestyle/hobbies_and_recreation/genealogy/

Excite includes the Broderbund Family Finder, searching pedigrees submitted by users of Family Tree Maker and also indexes on CDROM published by Broderbund. On most of the entries you just get told which CDROM a name appears on - you can then buy the CDROM or find someone else to do a lookup for you. It also searches web sites - not just genealogy ones.

SEARCHING OLD AND NEW MAILING LIST MESSAGES

```
> > > File 951030-161:
Article#6583 - Subject: Blackmores of Kent and London
Article#6583 - Subject: Blackmores of Kent and London
I am researching the family of BLACKMORE who seemed to originate in
I also have details of some other Blackmore researchers.
< < < End of matches in file 951030-161
```

Figure 12 One of four matches to: **search genuki-digest "Blackmore"**

Messages in most mailing lists are archived, and in some the archives can be searched for the occurrence of particular surnames, or place names. On page 8 I describe the operation of the mailing list Genuki-L. I went on to search it for the surname Blackmore. I sent a series of messages to the server. My message **help** obtained information about commands. My message **search genuki-digest "Blackmore"** obtained an abstract of each message containing the word "Blackmore", with file and message numbers; Figure 12 shows one of the four I obtained, message (article) 6583 in digest 951030-161, so my next message was **get genuki-digest 951030-161**. This obtained a file with the whole of a day's messages. I searched down in this to message 6583, shown in Figure 13.

```
----- Start of Article -----
Article#6583 - Subject: Blackmores of Kent and London
From: kward@lionet.co.uk (Keith Ward)

I am researching the family of BLACKMORE who seemed to originate in Tenterden in
Kent and on the nearby Isle of Oxney. they later moved to London and a branch moved
to Hertfordshire (Briggins Park).

I am interested in the Kent family who were living in the area about 1760C and in
London about 1780. Originally sheep farmers they then seemed to move into the linen
trade and became merchants in London.

I also have details of some other Blackmore researchers.

Keith Ward
Email kward@lionet.co.uk   or KeithWard@msn.com

----- End of Article -----
```

Figure 13 Message retrieved from archive by: **get genuki-digest 95030-161**

That search was within the archive of one particular mailing list. The method of doing this depends on the software in use - you can get instructions through the help and information messages for the list. But there are more general methods. The search engine **Deja News** at **www.dejanews.com/** indexes old messages in many newsgroups and mailing lists. The **Messear** system at **www.sdtek.com/messear/messear.htm** provides a service for searching new messages - you register your surname interests and receive emails when any of them appear in the lists being searched by Messear. You also receive notification of new entries to the Roots Surname List for your surnames. I joined Rootsweb as a sponsor for $24 per annum to be able to use Messear - there are other benefits as well, including being able to set up a mailing list for your surname or other interest.

EMAIL ADDRESS DIRECTORIES

Roots Surname List, GenServ and others give links to genealogists researching particular names. You can also look up a surname in the email equivalent of a telephone directory.

Steve Hawgood in Hong Kong looked up his surname in the CompuServe directory - which includes most of the subscribers to CompuServe. The only other Hawgood

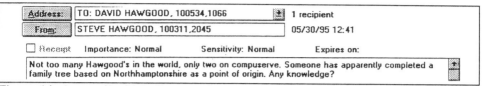

Figure 14. An email which discovered a seventh cousin once removed

subscriber he found was me. He sent me the email in Figure 14. I replied with an email giving my own ancestry back into Northamptonshire, and after a few more exchanges we established that he is my seventh cousin once removed. Our common ancestors were John Hawgood and Mary Lark, married in Northampton in 1702. Soon after this discovery, Kathryn Knight from *The Times* phoned me wanting examples of the way Internet is used for genealogy. The result was a half page story (on January 16th 1996) with photographs of me, Steve Hawgood in Hong Kong, the email which found the connection, the parish register entry for the 1702 marriage, and even the church in Northampton. The story also appeared in the Internet edition of *The Times*. As well as allowing me to recount the story, this does show that messages to namesakes can obtain results.

I have also tried a "white pages" directory in which anyone on Internet can have an entry, and I have entered my own details. It is *Internet Address Finder*. In January 1999 it has about 6 million entries. I tried searching for "Blackmore", as I had done on the genealogy lists. There were 78 Blackmore entries in this directory - probably 65 different people after eliminating those that were just alternative email addresses. I found this service returned results very quickly - well worth a try. It is on the Web at:
www.iaf.net/
WhoWhere?! at **www.whowhere.lycos.com/** combines searches for email addresses with searches of telephone directories - a useful set of searches.

TELEPHONE DIRECTORIES

There are some very good telephone directories on the Web - and many notable omissions. Australia (by state) and France (by town) are probably the best. For a list of phone directories look at:
http://home.wxs.nl/ ~ wvhwvh/ywpages.htm
www.teldir.com

I searched the phone directory for the state of Victoria in Australia for "Blackmore", there were too many to return. I refined the search to "J Blackmore" and found 16 in Melbourne, with addresses and phone numbers listed.